Can Rama Rajya Exist in Our Fast World?

A Mother's Answer to Her Daughter's Doubts

Ram SwaRajya

Think Tank Books

Title: Can Rama Rajya Exist in Our Fast World?
Author: Ram SwaRajya
Published by: Think Tank Books in 2025
Address: RZ-26/27B, Ashok Park, West Sagarpur, New Delhi - 110046
Website: thinktankbooks.com
Email: editorial@thinktankbooks.com

ISBN: 978-93-91607-16-6 / eISBN: 978-93-91607-48-7

Price: INR 120/-
Retail price listed is only for the Indian subcontinent.
Selling price may vary elsewhere.

Dedication

To India – for giving me life as a daughter first and then a mother.

And to you, the reader – thank you for taking the time to read this book.

Rama Rajya Begins With You

It was a bright morning. Birds were chirping outside the window, but inside the house, Vasantha was rushing. She had her college bag half-zipped, one shoe on, and was searching for her water bottle.

“Where are you going, Vasantha?” asked her mother, Mangalam, from the kitchen doorway.

“Maa,” Vasantha said, still searching for her bottle, “I really don’t understand you these days. Every time we talk, you somehow bring in *karma*, *dharma*, good deeds, and all these things from the past. Ever since I joined college, you have been trying to teach me some old value system that, frankly, doesn’t exist in today’s world. Maa, it’s the 21st century!”

"Now people only want to make money, get a good job, earn a big name, and live life the way they want. No one has time for all these 'ancient' principles. When you suddenly start talking about them in the middle of our normal conversations, I feel like walking away. I'm sorry, but I just can't take it anymore."

Vasantha finally found her bottle, stuffed it into her bag, and looked at her mother — expecting her to be upset.

But Mangalam did not look hurt. She did not argue. She simply smiled and even laughed a little.

"Maa? Why are you smiling? Didn't you hear what I just said?" Vasantha asked, completely confused.

Mangalam came closer and placed a hand on her daughter's shoulder. "I heard you, Vasanthu. And I understand you more than you think. When I was your age, I used to feel exactly the same way about my parents. I thought they were stuck in the past when they told me to be honest, kind, and fair. I thought the world was too fast and practical for such things."

"But you know what I learned over time? Those principles are not old-fashioned. They are like the foundation of a building. The design of the building can change, the colour can change, but without the foundation, it will fall."

Vasantha frowned. "Maa, I don't get it. You're talking about buildings and foundations — can you give me examples that actually make sense to my life?"

Mangalam laughed. "Alright, here's your life in your own language:

Remember last month, when your friend forgot her wallet in the canteen? You paid for her quietly and didn't tell anyone so she wouldn't feel embarrassed. That's ***compassion***.

Remember your exam last semester? You didn't copy from your friend, even though you knew you might get fewer marks. That's ***integrity***.

And remember the junior student in college who was being teased? You stepped in and told the seniors to stop. That's ***standing up for the weak***.

These things — they are exactly what I call *dharma*. You are already living them, you just don't call them by that name."

Vasantha stopped zipping her bag. "So... you mean *I* am already following your so-called old principles?"

Mangalam nodded. "Yes. Rama Rajya is not about a king sitting on a throne. It's about people — common people — living by truth, fairness, kindness, and responsibility.

Imagine this, Vasanthu:

A home where no one lies to each other.

A society where the poor are helped, not cheated.

Leaders who care about people instead of controlling them.

Friends and family who speak the truth, even when it's difficult.

People who choose the right thing over the easy thing, even when no one is watching.

That, my dear, is Rama Rajya. And it can exist even in 2025 — not as a kingdom, but as a way of life. You don't need a palace to build it. You can start with your own actions, in your own circle. One honest word, one kind act, one fair decision at a time."

For the first time, Vasantha didn't feel like her mother was giving her a lecture. Instead, she felt like she had been given a secret map — one that could work at any time, any place, even in her busy, modern life.

She smiled faintly, and for the rest of the day, her mother's words stayed with her like a small light in her heart.

A Week Later

It was a Thursday afternoon in college. The class had just finished, and the students were getting ready to leave when the professor made an announcement:

“There’s a missing phone in this classroom. If anyone finds it, please bring it to me.”

A few students laughed and joked about keeping it if they found it. Others didn't show any interest and walked away.

Vasantha was packing her bag when she noticed something shiny under a desk. She bent down and it was the missing phone. For a moment, she thought, No one is watching... I could easily keep this, or even sell it.

But then she remembered her mother's words: "People who choose the right thing over the easy thing, even when no one is watching — that's dharma."

She stood up, walked to the professor, and handed over the phone.

The professor smiled. "Thank you, Vasantha. The owner will be relieved."

Later that day, the phone's owner — a shy first-year student — came up to her with teary eyes and said, "Thank you, Didi (sister). My father bought this for me after saving for months."

As she walked away, Vasantha felt a warmth inside her. She realised her mother was right — Rama Rajya didn't need palaces or kings. It could start with a small act in a classroom, and it could start with her.

"Shri Ram Jai Ram Jai Jai Ram,

Jai Hanuman Gyan Gun Sagar"

(Glory to Lord Rama, Victory to Lord Rama, All Victory to Lord Rama;

Victory to Lord Hanuman, the ocean of wisdom and virtue).

A Note from the Author

In the Spirit of Rama Rajya

This book is part of a dream — not just of writing, but of building a 11,000-year legacy of wisdom, compassion, and truth.

I dedicate this work to the spirit of Rama Rajya — the golden age of righteousness, where justice reigned, truth prevailed, and no one suffered in silence.

Like Lord Rama, may we walk the path of Dharma, even when it's difficult. May this book carry light, honesty, and healing wherever it goes.

If you're reading this — you are part of this legacy now. Thank you for witnessing my words, my life, and my soul.

"May every home be an Ayodhya. May every heart be Rama's temple. May truth live forever."

With love and service,

Ram SwaRajya

(The kind of Self-love, care for others, and power for a right and good living based on Rama's values).

About the Author

Ram SwaRajya writes with a heartfelt purpose — to awaken the wisdom of India's timeless heritage in the hearts of today's generation.

The stories are not distant tales of saints or unreachable ideals, but living journeys of ordinary families — fathers, mothers, sons, and daughters — who discover spiritual truths in the flow of daily life. They remind us that true spirituality is not found only in temples or pilgrimages, but in the love, faith, and compassion we share with one another each day.

The name Ram SwaRajya carries the dream of Rama Rajya — a world rooted in truth, justice, peace, and compassion. Writing under this name, the author chooses simplicity over fame and sincerity over style, offering words as a light for every home and every heart.

Each page is written not just to be read, but to be felt — carrying the fragrance of devotion, the warmth of humanity, and the healing power of truth. The vision is simple: may every home become an Ayodhya, and every heart a temple of Ram.

A Kindness Note from the Author

While writing this fictional book, the author was supported by a bank loan. Driven by pure love and hope for world peace, a personal decision was made to share this book freely with everyone.

The author writes under the pen name Ram SwaRajya and is not seeking recognition, awards, or celebration in the community of book authors. There is no intention to follow formal publishing formats or societal expectations. Living as a common person and writing freely allows full creative liberty and the freedom to express the heart without limitations.

For readers who wish to support the author, bank details will be included in printed copies distributed by the author for free. For eBooks, the price is set by the publishing house, and readers do not need to make any payments to the author.

The author believes that your love, prayers, and presence are more than enough to support this work and its journey. Any future needs for support will be shared through upcoming books in this series.

If readers still wish to contact the author, they may write to:
ramswarajya2025@gmail.com